PRAISE FOR
THE CONFIDENCE CODE FOR GIRLS

"Girl power depends on self-confidence, but many girls struggle to see how awesome they really are. The good news is there are steps girls can take to build their confidence—not by twisting themselves into knots, but by gaining new mental tools and embracing their authentic selves. I wish I had this book when I was a girl—and I'm really glad today's girls have it now."

—SHERYL SANDBERG, COO of Facebook and
founder of Lean In and Option B

"This is the book every girl needs to make her dreams come true."

—LAURIE HERNANDEZ, US Olympic gold medalist and
bestselling author of *I Got This: To Gold and Beyond*

"An essential read for every girl in her tween years. This book encourages girls to take action despite unhelpful thinking patterns, to be unafraid of failure, and to challenge the worries that hold so many girls back. Presented in a relatable and engaging manner, it also provides excellent guidance on navigating the often judgmental and provoking world of social media. Girls will develop a much deeper understanding of what it means to be themselves and express that confidently. I am inspired by what the authors have done in offering such a tremendous guidebook that girls will reference time and time again in their journey to forming a solid, confident self."

—DR. BONNIE ZUCKER, licensed psychologist and author of
Anxiety-Free Kids: An Interactive Guide for Parents and Children

"If you've ever wished you had the courage to say what you really think, or do the thing that scares you, this is the book for you! Confidence is crucial for girls today, and Katty and Claire have figured out the recipe. Their advice is realistic and practical. Reading this book will help you change your life—and the world!"

—RACHEL SIMMONS, *New York Times* bestselling author of *Enough As She Is*, *Odd Girl Out*, and *The Curse of the Good Girl* and leadership expert at Smith College

"Girls should know it's cool to be different. I learned that lesson on the ice, playing hockey. I didn't always fit in, but I came to embrace that, and it gave me confidence. This book can help every girl flip that switch in her head, so she can feel the awesomeness and confidence that come from being unique."

—HILARY KNIGHT, Olympic gold medalist and member of the US women's national ice hockey team

"Wow!!! I love love love this book for girls. Every single day I work with girls who suffer so much because they don't have the tools *The Confidence Code for Girls* provides. It gives tweens tips and tools to manage everything from stress to self-doubt to sticky social situations. Adults will appreciate the book's focus on empowerment and concrete action steps, and girls will love the humor, stories, and fun activities. Whether you're a parent or an educator, this is an invaluable resource."

—PHYLLIS L. FAGELL, school counselor, author, and contributor to the *Washington Post*'s On Parenting column

THE CONFIDENCE CODE FOR GIRLS JOURNAL

A Guide to Embracing Your Amazingly
Imperfect, Totally Powerful Self

KATTY KAY & CLAIRE SHIPMAN

WITH JILLELLYN RILEY

HARPER
An Imprint of HarperCollinsPublishers

Library of Congress Control Number: 2019944884
ISBN 978-0-06-295410-7

20 21 22 23 PC/LSCC 10 9 8 7 6 5 4 3 2
❖
First Edition

Dear Reader,

If you're holding this book in your hands, you're obviously interested in building more confidence. First of all, GO YOU! Also, you've come to the right place. We've been studying confidence in women and girls for years and, through our research, we've cracked the code for confidence.

Confidence is what you need in order to try things, to do things, to take risks, to even just be yourself. It's really, really important. Luckily, it's not something that you either have or don't. We all start out with some, and we've discovered that you can actually MAKE more. The more new things you try, the more confidence you create! Sometimes, though, taking those confidence-building risks can be hard, especially for girls. Because a lot of women and girls really, really don't want to fail. We feel like we have to be perfect, all the time. But those kinds of thoughts create a lot of stress and anxiety, which leads to not trying anything new or different or cool.

Confidence helps us reject the negative voices in our heads, the ones that say:

It helps us focus on the positive voices that say, "You can totally do this!" and "Go for it!" so we can take action. But how do you get enough confidence to begin that cycle? Picking up this journal is a great place to start.

Our book *The Confidence Code for Girls* was a fun, important guide to building confidence for girls, full of great stories and helpful information. But to build confidence, you have to do more than just read about it. So we really wanted to create a place for you to map your own confidence journey. When you draw and write and make lists and doodle your fears and dreams—you're really crafting your own unique brand of confidence.

This journal will guide you through taking risks, dealing with setbacks, identifying strengths and weaknesses, and ditching the whole crazy, impossible idea of being perfect. Some pages will help you come up with things to tell yourself when you feel scared or overwhelmed. On others, you can list the times when you feel the most confident, so you can remind yourself later. And others will help you think about who you are and how to share your true self with the world—then turn those thoughts into reality.

Use this journal as a place where you can mess up, try again, cross things out, write something else, and come up with wild, incredible dreams for you to pursue. It's a place for you to create your most authentic, perfectly imperfect, and fully confident self.

We can't wait to see what you do with it.

Katty, Claire, and Jillellyn

con✳fi✳dence:

THAT INCREDIBLE ENERGY
WHEN YOU FIND
your courage
AND TRY
SOMETHING THAT'S NOT EASY.

It gives you the

POWER

to be yourself and
do what you want—
EVEN WHEN IT'S SCARY.

How does confidence make you feel?

Circle your top three.

strong

Amazing

Awesome

Unstoppable

Brave

Beautiful

Happy

Bold

Smart

cool

DO YOU THINK YOU ARE A CONFIDENT PERSON?

Why or why not?

WRITE ABOUT YOUR MOST CONFIDENT MOMENTS.
Go on, it's okay to brag.

when I play sports.

when I wear my favorite jeans.

when I do my best on a quiz.

Name five celebrities you admire who you think
glow with confidence.
(Yes, you're allowed to write Beyoncé more than once.)

 1

 2

 3

 4

 5

1. There's a cool new girl in your class and you want to be friends with her. Do you:

    a. "Accidentally" bump into her so you have a reason to talk to her?

    b. Casually start a conversation?

    c. Invite her to sit with you at lunch?

    d. Wait for her to talk to you?

2. You went shopping with your favorite cousin. She convinced you to buy a dress that you love but doesn't look like anything your classmates wear. Do you:

    a. Wear it only when you are hanging out with your cousin?

    b. Try it out with your friends on a weekend?

    c. Wear it to school—it looks great on you!

    d. Hang it in your closet but probably not wear it?

3. Your family is really into sports. But no matter which one you try, you just don't enjoy it. Do you:

    a. Keep playing—it will make everyone happy?

    b. Let your family know that next season will be your last?

    c. Quit playing and figure out what you want to do next?

    d. Play badly and hope they suggest you quit?

4. You love drawing and your parents think you have the talent to be an artist. Do you:

    a. Keep your sketchpads private?

    b. Share them with your close friends?

    c. Post your favorite sketch on social media?

    d. Hope your art teacher notices your work?

5. You hear your friends talking about going to the beach. They don't invite you but you want to go. Do you:

    a. Hang around, hoping they ask you to come?

    b. Ask one of your friends if you can go too?

    c. Send a group text asking about the plans?

    d. Throw out hints that you have nothing to do that day?

Answers:

Give yourself one point for every A or D answer, and four points for every B or C answer. If your score is thirteen or below, consider practicing your assertiveness; don't be afraid to speak your mind or step into the spotlight. If your score is fourteen or above, you're kicking butt at making your desires and talents known. Keep it up!

MAKE A LIST OF THINGS THAT ARE REALLY HARD or SCARY FOR YOU TO DO.

Say no to a friend.

Dance in public.

Answer questions in class.

This star means you'll come back to this page later on!

NOW, MAKE A LIST OF THINGS YOU'RE GOOD AT OR THAT MAKE YOU HAPPY.

Draw a picture of someone looking confident. Don't worry about making it perfect—this is just for you!

IF YOU COULD CHANGE *three things* IN YOUR LIFE THAT MAKE IT HARDER FOR YOU TO HAVE CONFIDENCE, WHAT WOULD THEY BE?

1 _____

_____

_____

_____

2 _____

_____

_____

_____

3 _____

_____

_____

_____

SCIENTISTS BELIEVE THAT
YOU CAN ACTUALLY

MAKE CONFIDENCE.

WHEN YOU TAKE ACTION,
ESPECIALLY WHEN YOU DO SOMETHING
EVEN SLIGHTLY RISKY,

YOU NOT ONLY

USE

CONFIDENCE, BUT YOU ALSO END UP

CREATING MORE!

Imagine some gears in your head. **confidence** is the grease that helps you turn those gears of your thoughts and generate action. And the fabulous result? That action generates more confidence for next time.

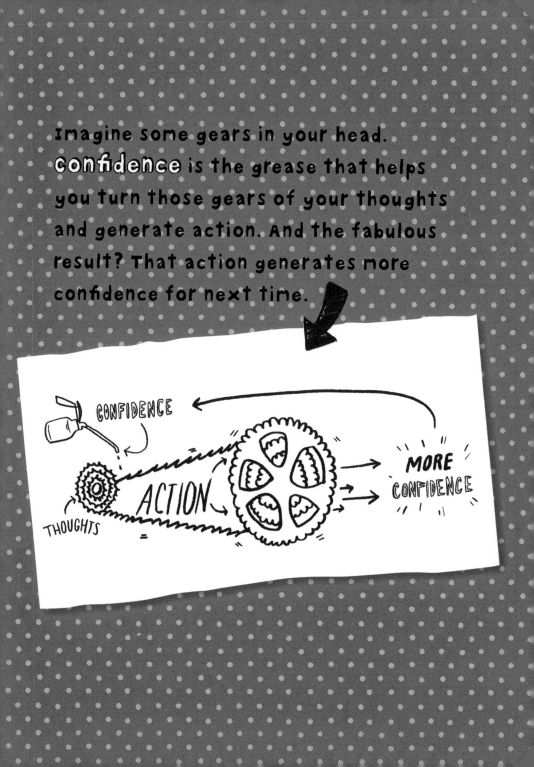

TAKING RISKS CAN BE SCARY.
CIRCLE THE RISKS THAT FRIGHTEN YOU THE MOST. BE HONEST!

Answering
a question
in class.

Running a
marathon.

Sitting at
a new table
for lunch.

Wearing
whatever
you want.

Inviting
someone you're
not really
friends with to
come over.

Saying
anything
at all ever
in public.

Singing a
solo in choir.

Posting an
unfiltered
selfie on
social media.

Playing a new
sport.

Sharing a
poem you
wrote.

Joining a club
where you
don't know
anyone.

Telling a
waiter he got
your order
wrong.

LOOK AT THE RISKS YOU CIRCLED. DO YOU SEE ANY COMMON THEMES?
WHY DO YOU THINK THOSE RISKS SCARE YOU THE MOST?

I'm afraid of being laughed at.

I'm scared of getting physically hurt.

What are *three things* you've done in the last year that have helped make you more *confident?*

MAKE A LIST OF CONFIDENT ROLE MODELS FROM YOUR OWN LIFE. WHAT ABOUT THEM DO YOU ADMIRE?

come back to this list whenever
you need inspiration!

WHAT MAKES YOU NERVOUS?

Everyone considers different things risky. What might be easy for one person makes another person really nervous. Take the quiz below, then add up the numbers next to your answers to see what kind of risks are hardest for you to tackle.

1. What scares you the most?

1. Auditioning for a play
2. Having an argument with your BFF
3. Hiking an unfamiliar trail

2. Which of these would you want to do the LEAST?

1. Present a report in front of the class
2. Share a poem with your friends
3. Ride a zip line down a hill

3. You get most nervous when you imagine:

1. Singing a solo in choir.
2. Sitting next to someone you don't know on the bus.
3. Trying to surf for the first time.

4. Which of these stresses you out the most?

1. Raising your hand in class
2. Hanging out with new people
3. Jumping off of a high dive

5. Do your palms sweat when you think about:

1. Running for student council?
2. Eating lunch by yourself?
3. Skateboarding in the park?

Answers:

If your score is close to four, then performance-based risks are super difficult for you. If your score is close to eight, then sharing your true self with the world makes you the most nervous. If your score is close to twelve, then physical risks are your biggest challenge.

Now that you know what risks scare you, how are you going to overcome them?

WHO'S YOUR MOST CONFIDENT FRIEND?

WHAT MAKES THEM SO CONFIDENT?

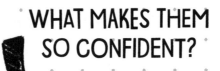

Imagine you're the most confident, SELF-ASSURED person you know, COMPLETELY UNAFRAID to do or say anything. What would you do? What would you say?

Talk to the new girl.

"umm . . . the way you're making fun of that kid isn't cool."

Try out for volleyball.

Research shows that when you compliment someone, you get a boost of confidence! Brainstorm some thoughtful compliments for people in your life and then share them!

PERSON: Ava

COMPLIMENT: You were awesome at our climate change

conference today. You're really good at debating with people!

How did you feel afterward? Warm and smiley

PERSON:

COMPLIMENT:

How did you feel afterward?

PERSON:

COMPLIMENT:

How did you feel afterward?

NOW WRITE SOME COMPLIMENTS TO YOURSELF!

LEARNING TO

TAKE RISKS

SO THAT YOU CREATE MORE CONFIDENCE DOESN'T MEAN

TAKING ALL RISKS.

• •

IT MEANS
TAKING SMART RISKS.

• •

SMART RISKS ARE THINGS THAT MIGHT SCARE YOU BUT,

in your gut,

YOU KNOW COULD INCREASE THE

FUN & ADVENTURE

IN YOUR LIFE.

Write some examples of smart and not-so-smart risks below.

SMART RISKS

Raising my hand in class, even when I'm not sure of the answer.

Singing a solo in choir.

DUMB RISKS

Hiking a new trail alone without telling anyone.

Cheating on a test.

RISKY BUSINESS

How good are you at telling the difference between risks that will add fun and confidence to your life and risks that are just plain dumb? circle the risks that seem like smart choices:

 Shooting a three-pointer from half court to beat the buzzer.

 Submitting your artwork to a public art show.

 Going with friends into an abandoned house.

 Asking your coach if you can play a new position.

 Texting a friend during a test.

 Staying out late without letting your parents know.

Hanging out with a new group of friends after school.

 Volunteering to lead a discussion in class.

Trying out for the school debate club.

 Dyeing part of your hair bright purple.

 Going to a new restaurant you've never tried.

 Riding the biggest roller coaster in the park.

Answers:

All of these are smart risks except for 3, 5, and 6. An abandoned house is not just risky—it can be really dangerous. You can get in a lot of trouble with the other two choices—so not worth it. Number 10 might not seem like a smart risk at first, but with your parents' permission, trying a new style is a great way to figure out what look makes you feel the most like your true self.

MAKE A LIST OF SMART RISKS YOU WANT TO TAKE, BIG AND SMALL. THEN CIRCLE THE ONE YOU WANT TO TAKE THE MOST.

For inspiration, look back at the list of things that are tough for you on page 8.

WHAT ARE THREE THINGS YOU'RE AFRAID COULD HAPPEN IF YOU TOOK YOUR CIRCLED RISK?

1

_____

_____

_____

_____

2

_____

_____

_____

3

_____

_____

_____

Here's another way to think about confidence—imagine it as a tiny, inspiring coach inside your mind, encouraging you to do all the things you want to do. Now jot down what that **CONFIDENCE COACH** would say to you!

YOU WON'T KNOW UNTIL YOU TRY!

DON'T GIVE UP!

YOU'VE GOT THIS!

FACE YOUR FEARS!

COACH

Now go find some real
CONFIDENCE COACHES!

ASK YOUR PARENTS, TEACHERS, AND FRIENDS FOR THEIR BEST
CONFIDENCE-BOOSTING ADVICE AND JOT IT DOWN HERE.

WE ALL HAVE OUR **COMFORT ZONES.** PLACES WHERE WE
KNOW WHAT'S UP AND FEEL TOTALLY COMFORTABLE—NO RISK INVOLVED!
BUT THERE'S NO CONFIDENCE BUILDING GOING ON THERE, EITHER.
DRAW SOME ACTIVITIES AND PLACES THAT ARE FIRMLY IN YOUR COMFORT ZONE.

NEED SOME IDEAS?
TURN BACK TO THE LIST OF THINGS YOU'RE GOOD AT ON PAGE 9.

NOW IMAGINE THAT YOU STAY
IN YOUR COMFORT ZONE FOREVER
AND NEVER BRANCH OUT.

What would you miss out on?

Your comfort zone can be cozy and fun, but you have to get out of it to have new experiences! The best way to get yourself out of your comfort zone is to take baby steps. When you break a big challenge down into little steps, it's a lot more achievable. Go back to your circled risk on page 28. Or choose a totally new risk that you really want to try!

Risk:

_____

_____

_____

_____

Why do you want to try this risk?

_____

_____

_____

_____

What will this risk help you achieve?

_____

_____

_____

_____

RESEARCH SHOWS THAT WHEN YOU TAKE THE TIME TO WRITE DOWN A GOAL AND LOG YOUR PROGRESS, YOU ARE 50 PERCENT MORE LIKELY TO MAKE IT A REALITY.

Now break your risk into five little steps. Your first step should be something you're ready to do. Write the steps below!

1 Write your risk down. ✔

YOU'VE ALREADY FINISHED STEP ONE! WAY TO GO!

2

3

4

5

Now give that next step a try.

HOW DID IT GO?

_____

_____

_____

_____

HOW DID IT FEEL?

_____

_____

_____

_____

_____

Try the rest of your steps. What happened? Was it awesome or harder than you thought it would be?

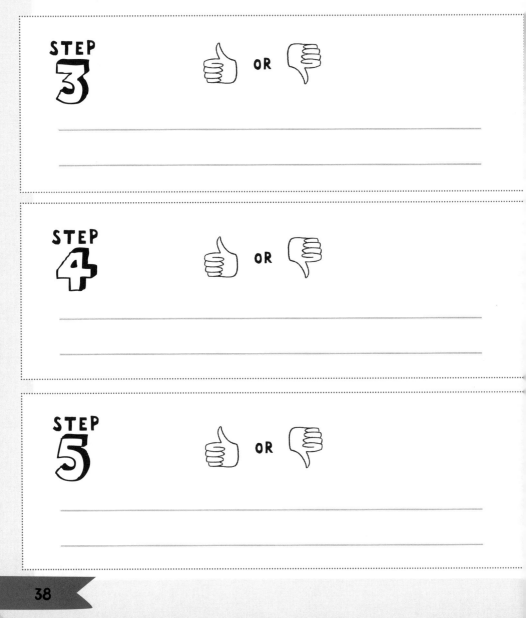

STEP
3

OR

_____
_____

STEP
4

OR

_____
_____

STEP
5

OR

_____
_____

Next time you try taking a risk, will you do anything differently? If so, what and why?

_____

_____

_____

_____

_____

_____

_____

_____

RESEARCH SHOWS THAT BY visualizing WHAT YOU want TO HAPPEN, YOU'RE MORE LIKELY TO make IT HAPPEN. Really! GIVE IT A TRY RIGHT NOW. CLOSE YOUR EYES. IMAGINE SOMETHING THAT YOU WANT AND believe IT WILL HAPPEN.

HERE ARE SOME CONFIDENCE-BOOSTING PHRASES YOU CAN USE WHEN YOU NEED A PEP TALK. TRY WRITING SOME OF YOUR OWN.

"It's okay to make a mistake."

"I've done stuff like this before and I can do it again."

"I'm proud of who I am."

confidence is a team sport!

Asking for help builds confidence, too.

Start a list of all the people you can count on, no matter what.

SOMETIMES ASKING FOR HELP CAN BE HARD. FOR EACH OF THE SITUATIONS BELOW, HOW COMFORTABLE WOULD YOU FEEL ASKING FOR HELP?

Asking your parents for advice about a situation with a friend

Asking for help would be:

1 2 3 4 5

EASY   MEH   HARD

How I would feel asking for help:

_____

_____

Asking a teacher to go over concepts you didn't understand after class

Asking for help would be:

1 2 3 4 5

EASY   MEH   HARD

How I would feel asking for help:

_____

_____

Asking your friend to help you organize a fundraiser you agreed to lead

Asking for help would be:

1 2 3 4 5

EASY   MEH   HARD

How I would feel asking for help:

_____

_____

Asking your coach to spend extra time practicing with you

Asking for help would be:

1 2 3 4 5

EASY   MEH   HARD

How I would feel asking for help:

_____

_____

Do you find it easy or hard to ask for help when things go wrong?

FAILURE FEELS TERRIBLE,
BUT BELIEVE IT OR NOT,

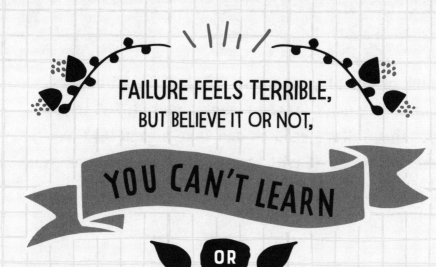

YOU CAN'T LEARN

OR

CREATE CONFIDENCE
without messing up sometimes!

WHENEVER YOU TAKE A RISK,
THERE'S A CHANCE IT MIGHT NOT GO WELL.
But that's okay—failure is a part of
BUILDING
CONFIDENCE.

Think of one of your worst failures. A big one. Of course, you don't want to think about it. But if you face that failure head on and take a good look at what happened, it will have way less power over you.

Write about that failure—what happened, how it felt, and how you dealt with it.

Talk to yourself about that failure like you would talk to a friend who did the same thing. What would you say to make her feel better?

WHAT DO YOU DO TO FEEL BETTER AFTER SOMETHING BAD HAPPENS? CIRCLE YOUR TOP THREE!

Try to figure out what went wrong.

Sob into my pillow.

Listen to music really loud.

Read a book.

Dive back in and give it another try.

Eat tons of ice cream.

Talk to a friend.

Ask myself what I'll do differently next time.

Write in a journal.

Remind myself everybody messes up sometimes.

Go for a run.

Talk to a trusted adult.

Think of ways that life could be worse.

CAN YOU THINK OF SOMETHING YOU USED TO BE BAD AT DOING? WRITE ABOUT HOW YOU GOT BETTER AT IT OVER TIME.

HOW DO YOU DEAL WITH AN EPIC FAIL?

1. You thought you totally aced a math quiz. But when you get it back, you didn't just do badly—you actually got an F! How do you react?

a) You sleepwalk through your day until you can go home and crawl into bed.

b) Why didn't you study more? That was so stupid.

c) You cry. And cry. And cry. You are definitely going to fail the class—so you cry some more.

d) It's one quiz, not your grade for the semester. You can fix it, but it's going to take some extra studying.

2. You make plans with a friend, only to bail at the last minute because you aren't feeling it. She texts back that she's tired of you always canceling, and she's done trying to hang out with you. How do you feel?

a) Thank you, next. You don't need uptight friends.

b) How could you be such a jerk? She's right to drop you. You're a terrible friend.

c) She's going to tell your friends, who are going to take her side. Everyone is going to hate you!

d) She's right to be upset. You give it a little time, then go to her house to say you're sorry.

3. **You agree to dog sit for your neighbor while they are on vacation. You forget to lock the gate to the living room and the dog chews on the leg of the couch. What do you do?**

a) Don't mention it and hope they don't notice.

b) You can't be trusted. Never dog sit again.

c) Arrange not to be there when they get back—they're going to be absolutely furious. What if they make you pay for the couch?

d) Let them know when they get home, apologize, and ask what you can do to make it better.

Answers:

If you picked mostly **A**s, you're a denier. You try to pretend like nothing is wrong—which can actually create more problems. If you picked mostly **B**s, you tend to beat yourself up for your failures. Remember to treat yourself like a friend—everyone messes up sometimes! If you picked mostly **C**s, one little failure has you going "I'm completely doomed!" You tend to jump to the worst conclusion right away and think you can never fix things. And if you picked mostly **D**s, you tend to accept what went wrong and focus on how to do better next time.

IF YOU AREN'T WILLING TO FAIL, YOU'LL BE TOO SCARED TO TAKE RISKS. WHICH MEANS YOU'LL NEVER BECOME YOUR MOST CONFIDENT SELF!

Draw or list some ways to boost your mood and get your brain to a better place after something goes wrong.

Go back to the list of role models you made on page 17. Dig around for cool failure stories, either on the internet if they're famous or by asking if it's someone you know. Odds are you'll find some—everyone, including every successful person, has failed at some point!

write them below.

You've got to find a way to laugh when disaster strikes! Make an "It Could Be Much Worse" list and write down how your big failure could have been more awful—like maybe if you'd forgotten to put on pants or an elephant fell on your head.

1.

2.

3.

4.

5.

SOMETIMES, IT'S EASY TO

overthink things.

YOU MESS ONE THING UP
AND SUDDENLY YOU'RE SURE THAT YOU'RE A

COMPLETE FAILURE.

EVERYONE KNOWS IT AND EVERYONE HATES YOU.

YOU JUST CAN'T STOP THINKING ABOUT IT.

>>> THAT'S CALLED RUMINATING <<<

and it can be a major confidence killer.

TOO MUCH THINKING CAN MAKE YOU LESS LIKELY TO

DO & TRY & RISK.

I let everyone
down.

Everyone
hates me.

Everyone is
laughing at me.

This is the worst
mistake ever.

I'm a failure at
everything.

I'm a terrible
person.

Those girls are
whispering. And I'm
sure it's about ME!

I'll never be good
at anything.

There's no way I
can fix this.

This is horrible
and there's nothing
I can do.

THINK ABOUT A TIME SOMETHING BAD HAPPENED AND YOU
COULDN'T STOP THINKING ABOUT IT, OVER AND OVER.

Write down some of those thoughts.

Did you notice how, just by remembering your negative thoughts, you FELT sad or angry or really down? Now, think about a time you did something totally awesome. Try to relive that moment. Write about how it felt.

REMEMBER THIS CONFIDENCE-BUILDING FORMULA: WHAT WE THINK CREATES WHAT WE FEEL, WHICH THEN SHAPES WHAT WE DO.

HAVE YOU EVER SKIPPED SOMETHING COOL OR FUN BECAUSE YOU WERE WORRIED ABOUT WHAT MIGHT HAPPEN?

HOW DID YOU FEEL ABOUT MISSING OUT?

WHAT WERE YOU AFRAID WOULD HAPPEN IF YOU DECIDED TO DO IT?

Imagine your best friend is a big overthinker. Try giving her a pep talk and some ideas of what she can do to make these situations better.

situation

I failed my history test! What if I fail the whole class? What if I don't get into a good college?

Pep Talk _____

_____

_____

Ideas _____

_____

_____

_____

situation

I missed the big goal in my soccer game. I totally let my team down. I'm just terrible at soccer. I should quit.

Pep Talk _____

_____

_____

Ideas _____

_____

_____

Situation

I talked about how much I love my favorite TV show with some girls I don't know that well and they all said it's for little kids. They think I'm totally boring and stupid now. Why did I ever try to talk to them?

Pep Talk _____

_____

_____

Ideas _____

_____

_____

_____

Situation

I accidentally sent a text complaining about Sofia . . . to Sofia! It's so embarrassing. She's going to hate me forever. Our friendship is totally over!

Pep Talk _____

_____

_____

Ideas _____

_____

_____

QUIZ
WHERE DOES YOUR HEAD GO?

1. You drop a full lunch tray in front of the whole cafeteria. BAM! Heads turn and food flies everywhere. Do you think:

a. I need to leave school RIGHT. THIS. MINUTE. I can never eat lunch in the cafeteria again.

b. That popular girl is laughing—she's going to tell everyone what a loser I am.

c. I'm always such an embarrassment. I'm never going to live this down.

d. This stinks! Maybe by the time I finish cleaning up, everyone will be back to eating their lunch.

2. You're at a party with a lot of older kids. You make a joke and start cracking up . . . then realize you're the only one laughing. Do you think:

a. I need to go hide in the bathroom and text my mom to come get me!

b. These kids are never, ever going to be my friends now.

c. I'm always going to be known as the dork who thinks she's funny.

d. Maybe I should take a deep breath and then try to jump back into the conversation.

3. **You forgot to practice the new song for band. You make a ton of mistakes and your music teacher calls you out on it in front of everyone. Do you think:**

   a. I'm going to have to quit band.

   b. My teacher thinks I'm terrible. Everyone in band is so tired of me messing up.

   c. How am I ever going to learn this song? I'll never get it right!

   d. I really need to practice more before the next rehearsal.

4. **You are playing goalie in soccer. In the third quarter, the other team scores an easy goal, one you should have stopped. Do you think:**

   a. I just lost the game for us.

   b. My coach is so mad. He's going to pull me.

   c. I'm definitely going to be riding the bench for the rest of the season.

   d. The game's not over yet. I'd better get ready for the next shot.

Answers:

Of all these reactions, only D is actually grounded in reality. The others are flawed thinking patterns, where you A assume the worst, B think you know what other people are thinking, or C feel like you can't change the future. When you let your thoughts get carried away like that, you usually end up feeling way worse than before. But by noticing what patterns your flawed thinking tends to take, you can make sure to watch out for those flawed thinking habits next time you fall into a ruminating spiral.

You have a lot on your mind! The more you have to juggle, the easier it can be to start worrying about things. write or draw some of the things on your mind lately in the brain below.

One of the best ways to stop yourself from overthinking is to tell yourself the "Maybe" story. Think about a time you started overthinking because you made a mistake or did something embarrassing. Now create a new story about why maybe what happened wasn't so bad.

Maybe _____

_____

Maybe _____

_____

Maybe _____

> Maybe everyone was too distracted by pizza day to notice when I tripped.

_____

Maybe _____

_____

Maybe _____

> Maybe Kate was laughing at something on her phone, not at me.

Maybe _____

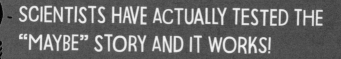

SCIENTISTS HAVE ACTUALLY TESTED THE "MAYBE" STORY AND IT WORKS!

WRITE DOWN SOME THINGS YOU'VE DONE THAT YOU'RE PROUD OF. THEY CAN BE SMALL OR BIG, PRAISED OR COMPLETELY UNNOTICED BY OTHERS. WHENEVER YOU FEEL DOWN, LOOK AT THIS LIST AS A REMINDER OF HOW MUCH YOU'VE ACHIEVED!

KEEP ADDING TO IT AS YOU ACCOMPLISH MORE!

LOOK AT THE LIST YOU JUST MADE OF YOUR ACCOMPLISHMENTS AND PICK ONE THAT MAKES YOU FEEL ESPECIALLY PROUD.

Now go ahead and brag.

WHAT DID YOU DO THAT WAS SO AWESOME?

HOW DID YOU DO IT?

HOW COOL IS THIS?

OUR BRAINS MIGHT OVERTHINK THINGS SOMETIMES,
BUT THEY CAN ACTUALLY BE REWIRED BY

DOING THINGS DIFFERENTLY.

which means every time you
stop yourself from overthinking,
it gets a little easier to stop next time.

PRETTY SOON, YOU'LL DO IT

AUTOMATICALLY.

When we start overthinking, it's easy to make things seem worse than they are. Write about a time that you overthought yourself into a spiral.

ONE OF THE BEST WAYS TO STOP A RUMINATING ATTACK IS TO KNOW WHAT TRIGGERS ONE!

Make a list of things that often lead to overthinking for you. That way, when it happens you can stop yourself and go, "Hey, I'm ruminating. Maybe I should take a break and come back to this later."

_____

_____

_____

_____

_____

_____

_____

_____

IF YOU NEED INSPIRATION, TRY LOOKING AT THE LISTS OF THINGS THAT ARE HARD FOR YOU AND THE LIST OF THINGS THAT YOU'RE GOOD AT ON PAGES 8 AND 9.

WHEN WAS THE LAST TIME YOU FELT
REALLY, REALLY HAPPY?

WHY?

Things That Make Me Happy

WHEN WE STARE AT POSITIVE IMAGES AND THINK POSITIVE THOUGHTS, WE RELEASE ENDORPHINS—A FEEL-GOOD HORMONE—THROUGHOUT OUR BODIES. SO LET'S MAKE A MINI MOOD BOARD THAT CAN GET THOSE ENDORPHINS FLOWING. GET OUT THE SCISSORS, GLUE, AND GLITTER. CUT AND PASTE IMAGES OR WORDS THAT REMIND YOU OF WHAT MAKES YOU HAPPY OR WHAT MAKES YOU FEEL REFRESHED AND RESTORED.

WHEN WAS THE LAST TIME YOU FELT REALLY, REALLY SAD?

_____

_____

_____

_____

WHY?

_____

_____

_____

_____

Write down all your negative thoughts and then scribble over them so hard you can't see them anymore. Scientists say that this actually helps you feel better!

Make a list of three things you're thankful for. Then repeat this every day! People who spend more time being grateful every day are happier and healthier.

DATE:

1 _____

2 _____

3 _____

DATE:

1 _____

2 _____

3 _____

DATE:

1 _____

2 _____

3 _____

Date:

1 _____

2 _____

3 _____

Date:

1 _____

2 _____

3 _____

Date:

1 _____

2 _____

3 _____

Date:

1 _____

2 _____

3 _____

List the times you feel the most stressed or worried and what thoughts you have then.

_____

_____

_____

_____

_____

_____

_____

_____

_____

_____

_____

_____

NOW LIST THE MOMENTS WHEN YOU FEEL THE MOST
relaxed & confident.

♥

♥

♥

♥

♥

♥

♥

♥

♥

♥

♥

LIST SOME PLACES WHERE YOU FEEL MORE CONFIDENT AND HAPPY
THAN OTHERS. THEN WRITE ABOUT THE THOUGHTS YOU HAVE WHEN
YOU'RE THERE.

_____

_____

_____

_____

_____

_____

_____

_____

_____

_____

_____

_____

DID YOU KNOW THAT

GOOD FRIENDSHIPS

HELP YOU LIVE LONGER AND MAKE YOU LESS STRESSED?

HAVING GOOD FRIENDS BOOSTS YOUR

CONFIDENCE

AND MAKES IT EASIER TO BE

YOUR **BEST** SELF.

WHAT MAKES SOMEONE A GOOD FRIEND?
Circle the three that are most important to you.

Fun

Lots of
inside jokes

Similar
interests

Smart

Loyal

Makes me laugh

Trustworthy

Kind

Makes me feel
better on a bad day

Understands
me

Keeps my
secrets

Supportive

Popular

Wears cool
clothes

WHY DO YOU THINK YOU'RE A GOOD FRIEND?

List a few reasons.

_____

_____

_____

_____

_____

_____

_____

_____

_____

MAKING AND KEEPING FRIENDS REQUIRES RISK-TAKING, CONFIDENCE, AND COMMUNICATION! IT'S A GREAT WAY TO BUILD UP YOUR CONFIDENCE SKILLS.

Friends can make you laugh and keep you sane. But sometimes a bad friend can make you feel terrible and doubt yourself. What are some warning signs that someone ISN'T a true friend?

"Doesn't listen to me."

"Makes fun of me."

"Pushes me to do things I don't want to do."

HAVE YOU EVER HAD A FRIEND WHO DIDN'T REALLY HAVE YOUR BEST INTERESTS AT HEART?

What advice would you give to someone in that situation?

WHAT'S YOUR FRIENDSHIP STYLE?

Are you a social butterfly, BFF, or part of a squad?

1. **If you had to describe what makes you a fun friend, you'd say:**
   a. "I help my group get along."
   b. "I always make time for some one-on-one."
   c. "I bring the fun."

2. **On the first day of school, who are you most psyched to see?**
   a. The girls you walk to school with
   b. Your bestie after school, so you can dissect your day
   c. All the people you didn't see over the summer

3. **You are most likely to hang out with girls:**
   a. You are in classes with this year.
   b. You've known forever.
   c. Who you recently met and like.

4. **Your mom says you can do something fun for your birthday. You have:**
   a. Your close crew for a sleepover. Who's up for truth or dare!?
   b. Mani-pedis for you and your BFF.
   c. A pool party with a giant game of "Marco Polo."

Answers:

If you answered mainly **A**s, you tend to hang with a core group of fun people. If you answered mainly **B**s, you prefer to spend time with one or two BFFS. If you answered mainly **C**s, you like knowing all kinds of people and have friends in a bunch of different groups.

TIME FOR A FRIENDSHIP CHECK-IN!

Answer true or false for the following statements.

I have good friends.

_____

I trust my friends.

_____

I feel like I am a good friend.

_____

When one of my friends hurts my
feelings, I feel like I can talk to her.

_____

If I tell a friend a secret, I know
she won't tell anyone else.

_____

My friends apologize when they
hurt my feelings.

_____

I apologize when I hurt my friends'
feelings.

_____

When my friends and I have issues,
we can work them out.

_____

My friends want me to succeed no
matter what.

_____

I want my friends to succeed no
matter what.

_____

**LOOK BACK AT YOUR ANSWERS. If you answered mostly true,
you and your friends are ride or die! If you answered mostly
false, you and your BFFs might need to talk some things out.**

DO YOU CONSIDER YOURSELF MORE OF A LEADER OR A FOLLOWER?

_____

_____

_____

_____

WHY?

_____

_____

_____

_____

Write about a time you were in a situation with a friend that you didn't know how to handle.

_____

_____

_____

_____

_____

What did you end up doing?

_____

_____

_____

_____

Do you think it was the right thing to do?

_____

_____

_____

_____

THINK OF A PROBLEM YOU'VE HAD WITH A FRIEND LATELY AND BREAK IT DOWN OVER THE NEXT FEW PAGES.

Problem:

How do you feel about this problem?

How do you think your friend feels about this problem?

can you think of any reasons why you might be having this problem?

WHEN YOU WORK OUT PROBLEMS WITH FRIENDS,
IT HELPS TO SHARE HOW YOU'RE FEELING. GOOD
FRIENDSHIPS ONLY GET STRONGER WHEN YOU CAN OPEN UP.

Write down some "I" statements about
your problem with your friend.

I _____

_____

I _____

_____

I _____

_____

I _____

_____

BRAINSTORM SOME SOLUTIONS TO THE PROBLEM YOU'RE HAVING WITH YOUR FRIEND.

NOW TRY PUTTING ALL THOSE STEPS INTO PRACTICE AND HAVING A CONVERSATION WITH YOUR FRIEND. USE THIS SCRIPT TO PLAN OUT WHAT YOU'RE GOING TO SAY IN ADVANCE.

❝ Hey, do you have a second? I want to talk about something.

(Tell her what's going on.)
The other day when _____

(Start with "I.")
I felt _____

(Own your part in the issue.)
I know that I _____

(Give your friend a chance to explain.)
Did you mean for that to happen?

(Find a compromise.)
Maybe next time we could _____
❞
_____

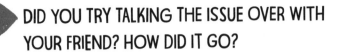 DID YOU TRY TALKING THE ISSUE OVER WITH
YOUR FRIEND? HOW DID IT GO?

WHAT WILL YOU DO DIFFERENTLY NEXT TIME?

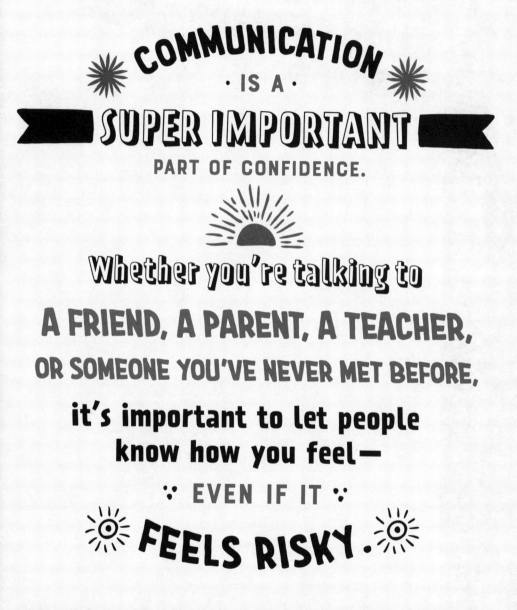

COMMUNICATION · IS A · **SUPER IMPORTANT** PART OF CONFIDENCE.

Whether you're talking to **A FRIEND, A PARENT, A TEACHER,** OR SOMEONE YOU'VE NEVER MET BEFORE, it's important to let people know how you feel— EVEN IF IT **FEELS RISKY.**

OU GENERALLY FEEL LIKE YOU'RE GOOD AT TALKING

OTHER PEOPLE WHEN THEY HURT YOUR FEELINGS?

Y OR WHY NOT?

_____

_____

_____

_____

_____

_____

_____

_____

_____

_____

_____

_____

_____

HAVE FRIENDS EVER COME TO YOU TO TALK ABOUT A TIME YOU HURT THEIR FEELINGS? HOW DID IT FEEL?

ARE YOU THE KIND OF PERSON WHO MAKES NEW FRIENDS
EASILY OR FINDS IT EASY TO TALK TO PEOPLE YOU
DON'T KNOW THAT WELL? WHY?

MEETING NEW PEOPLE IS SCARY! But making new friends is a great way to create confidence and have way more fun. Are there any people you want to be better friends with or groups you want to join?

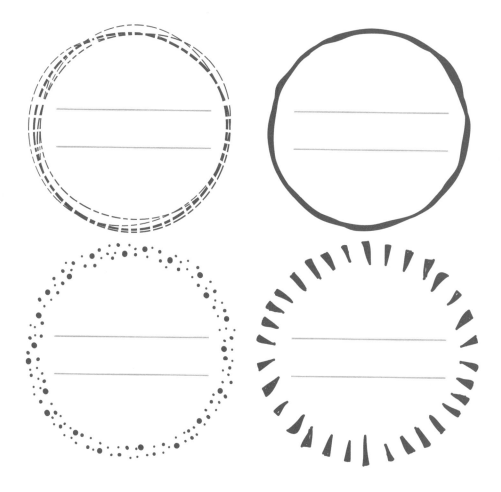

NOW BRAINSTORM SOME WAYS TO START MAKING NEW FRIENDS, LIKE ASKING THEM TO HANG OUT AFTER SCHOOL OR COMPLIMENTING SOMETHING SMART THEY SAID IN CLASS.

While it's fun to share cute videos and inside jokes with friends, being able to talk about how you feel and work through problems is what keeps friendships going. What do you do when things get awkward? Let's find out.

1. **You and Riley have been trick-or-treating on Halloween together since kindergarten. But this year, she wants to invite some new kids along that you don't know well. What do you do?**

   a. Say "sure" to hide your anger and hurt feelings, then have a miserable time on Halloween.

   b. Tell Riley to go with them, you'll make your own plans. Obviously, they're more important to her than you are now.

   c. Explain that you feel kind of silly saying it, but you always thought of Halloween as a tradition. Maybe you do a few houses together and meet up with the group a little later?

2. **One friend in your group has been really annoying lately. Every conversation has to be about her or she zones out on her phone. Your group is getting really sick of her and the texts are flying about what dumb thing she said today. What do you do?**

   a. Avoid her, so you don't have to feel guilty about it. It's not like you can change her personality.

b. Keep making fun of her. It's her fault she's being so rude!

c. Find a time to talk to her about her behavior. Use "I" instead of "You" statements, like "I've noticed people seem to be getting frustrated with you lately. Why do you think that is?" so it sounds less jerky.

3. Your older sister has been promising to go with you to see the sequel to your favorite movie. Then she goes opening weekend with her friends! How do you react?

a. Silently seethe and don't count on her for anything ever again.

b. Tell your mom, so she gets in trouble for not going with you.

c. Tell her that you were looking forward to going together and you're hurt.

Answers:

If you picked mostly **A**s, you tend to avoid problems in your friendships and hope they'll just go away. Unfortunately, these problems don't usually fix themselves.

If you answered **B**s, you tend to lash out when someone hurts your feelings. Instead of telling them that they're upsetting you, you're trying to upset them right back.

If you picked **C**s, you're communicating with your friends in an open and healthy way and expressing your feelings. It might be hard sometimes, but it's a great way to build confident friendships.

WE ALL KNOW BULLIES—PEOPLE WHO SEEM TO THRIVE ON MAKING OTHERS MISERABLE.

Have you ever been bullied? How did it feel?

_____

_____

_____

_____

_____

_____

_____

_____

_____

Write about a time you called someone a name or made a joke at someone else's expense. How did it make you feel? How do you think it made them feel?

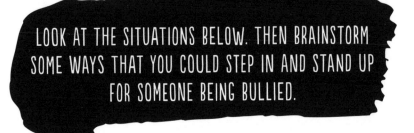

LOOK AT THE SITUATIONS BELOW. THEN BRAINSTORM SOME WAYS THAT YOU COULD STEP IN AND STAND UP FOR SOMEONE BEING BULLIED.

Situation: In the cafeteria, you see a group of people move Aliya's tray to a different table when she goes to the bathroom, and then tell her she has to eat alone because there's no more room for her.

Solution: _____

_____

_____

Situation: When Monica, a girl on your softball team, strikes out, some of your teammates start sarcastically yelling "Nice job" and telling her to quit the team.

Solution: _____

_____

_____

SOCIAL MEDIA, CELL PHONES THE INTERNET

can be the ultimate

CONFIDENCE BLACK HOLE,

making you wish you were living someone else's life instead of your own.

BUT IT'S IMPORTANT TO REMEMBER THAT SOCIAL MEDIA IS JUST A HIGHLIGHTS REEL— PEOPLE ONLY POST WHAT THEY MOST WANT YOU TO SEE.

Everyone has problems that they're sorting out off-camera.

Do social media and the internet
make you feel more stressed or
relaxed and happy?

 **Fun fact:** RESEARCHERS HAVE FOUND THAT THE SAME PART OF OUR BRAIN LIGHTS UP WHEN WE EAT CHOCOLATE **AND** WHEN WE GET LIKES ONLINE. NO WONDER IT'S SO FUN!

What I love about social media and life online:

Things about social media and the internet that aren't so cool:

Have you ever said something on social media or through text that you regret? What happened?

_____

_____

_____

_____

_____

_____

_____

_____

_____

_____

_____

_____

_____

_____

_____

DRAW A PICTURE OF YOURSELF IN REAL LIFE.

(Don't worry about your art skills—stick figures are perfectly fine!)

NOW DRAW A PICTURE OF YOURSELF THE WAY YOU SEEM ONLINE—OR HOW YOU *WANT* TO BE SEEN ONLINE.

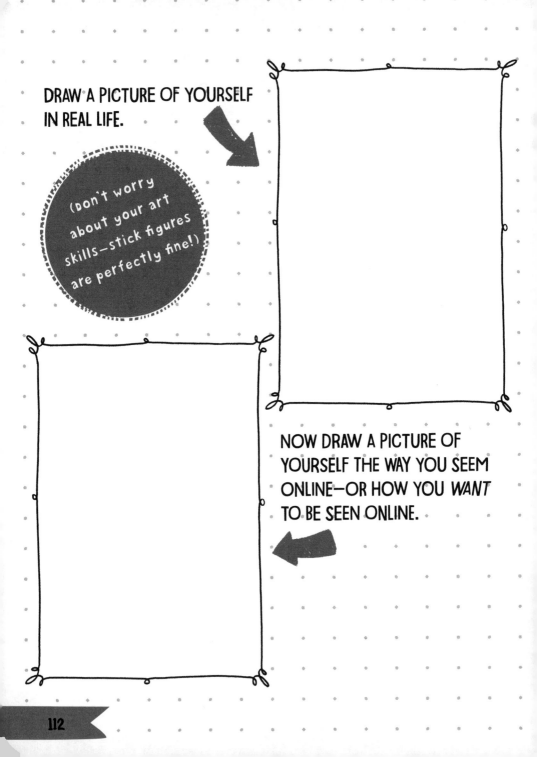

How do you think you act differently online?

_____

_____

_____

_____

_____

_____

_____

_____

Fact:

77 PERCENT OF TEENS THINK THEY ARE LESS AUTHENTIC AND REAL ONLINE THAN IN PERSON.

Does social media help you express your best self or make you feel like you're not enough? For each line, circle the adjective that feels right to you most of the time.

WHEN I SEE OTHER PEOPLE'S IMAGES AND POSTS ON SOCIAL MEDIA, I FEEL:

Empowered	or	self-conscious
confident	or	insecure
Beautiful	or	flawed
Happy with my body	or	unhappy with my body
Popular	or	unpopular
Fun	or	uncool

WHEN I POST ON SOCIAL MEDIA, I:

Feel funny	or	feel boring
Feel confident	or	feel self-critical
Do it just for fun	or	worry about the number of likes I get
Don't put in a lot of time, it's not that big a deal	or	spend a lot of time making it perfect before I post
Feel happy with myself	or	feel unhappy with myself
Act like myself	or	try to seem like a better version of myself

If you circled mostly the adjectives on the left, social media is boosting you up, not bringing you down! If you circled mostly the adjectives on the right, you might want to rethink the ways you're using social media.

ARE PEOPLE GENERALLY NICER TO EACH OTHER IN PERSON OR ONLINE?

List some reasons why you think that is.

>>>>>>>>>>>>>>>>>>>>>>>>>>>>>>>>>>

_____

_____

_____

_____

_____

_____

_____

_____

Does the time you spend on social media help your confidence or hurt it? Take the following quiz to see how screen time is affecting the way you feel.

1. You weren't paying attention and now your phone is dead. How do you feel until you can get it charged again?

a. Desperate! What if I miss something important?

b. A little strange. I keep reaching to check it, then remembering that I can't.

c. Whatever! I can go do something else.

2. A friend posts a group photo where you think you look weird. How do you react?

a. I'm furious! I only post photos where I look amazing. I have to text her and insist she take it down.

b. I'm a little annoyed. I'll ask my friend to show me the photo next time before posting.

c. No biggie—it's a group shot.

3. How do you feel when you see a photo of your friends hanging out without you?

a. It's like being punched. Why wasn't I included?

b. Two can play at that game. I immediately post a photo of me out with other friends.

c. It stings, but I don't always invite everyone every time to hang out either.

4. Have you ever sent a mean text about someone that you would never, ever want them to read?

a. Of course, everyone does. It's no big deal.

b. Only in group chats with my close friends.

c. I try not to ever do it.

5. Do you ever find yourself poring through someone's feed, wishing you could have all of their friends?

a. Sure, they all seem to have a great time.

b. Sometimes—it would be great to be so popular.

c. Online friends and real friends are two different things.

Answers:

If you picked mostly As, you might be addicted to your phone. Be careful—when you spend too much time on social media, your confidence can start to take a hit.

If you picked mostly Bs, you're a little obsessed with social media. It might be better for your confidence if you put the screen down more often.

If you picked mostly Cs, you're managing to keep a good balance between life online and life IRL. Remember to keep paying attention to that balance!

Think of some ways that you can encourage people to be nicer to each other online and jot some ideas down here.

_____

_____

_____

_____

_____

_____

_____

_____

_____

_____

Fact: 95 PERCENT OF TEENAGERS HAVE NOTICED BULLYING ONLINE.

What ways have you used the internet to boost your confidence and make you feel connected to people?

WHAT ARE YOUR TOP SOCIAL MEDIA TIPS?

"If I'm mad, I make myself wait before I send anything."

"Think before you hit send when it involves a picture.
Would you care if your grandma saw it?"

"Use all caps CAREFULLY! They can be FUN, or TOO MUCH!"

Do you ever feel like

YOU'RE NOT GOOD ENOUGH?

Are you constantly

COMPARING YOURSELF TO OTHERS

or thinking back over something you said,

wishing you could get a do-over?

You might be suffering from a case of

PERFECTIONISM.

>>>>>>>>>>>>>>>>>>>>>>>>>>>>>>>

Perfectionism is the feeling that you need to

GET EVERYTHING EXACTLY RIGHT.

It might seem like something to aim for, but since

PERFECTION IS IMPOSSIBLE,

it actually tears down your confidence
and makes you too afraid to

TAKE RISKS.

per*fec*tion*ism

Write your own definition of perfectionism.

_____

_____

_____

What seems good about trying to be perfect?

_____

_____

_____

Can you think of any ways that perfectionism might not be helpful?

_____

_____

_____

_____

ARE THERE ANY AREAS OF YOUR LIFE WHERE YOU FEEL PRESSURED TO DO EVERYTHING *JUST RIGHT*? IT CAN BE IN CLASS, AT HOME, ON YOUR INSTA, PRETTY MUCH ANYTHING. THESE ARE YOUR perfectionism pressures.

DOES PERFECTIONISM GET IN THE WAY OF YOUR DAY? FOLLOW THE ARROWS AND ANSWER THE QUESTIONS.

Do you ever feel like everything you try to do just isn't good enough?

How often do you compare yourself to others?
circle one.

A few times a month

A few times a day

A few times a week

A few times an hour

How does it feel?

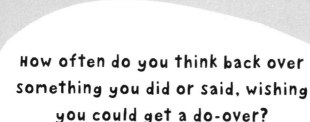

How often do you think back over something you did or said, wishing you could get a do-over?

WHEN YOU TRY TO BE PERFECT AND AREN'T WILLING TO FAIL, YOU CLOSE YOURSELF OFF TO TAKING RISKS OR ACTIONS. YOU CAN'T BE CONFIDENT THAT WAY!

IS PERFECTIONISM STRESSING YOU OUT?

Wouldn't your life be awesome if you could do everything just right—wear the coolest clothes, have terrific grades, be great at sports?

We all have things that we wish we were better at. Sometimes, though, we want to do well so badly, we end up sabotaging ourselves by trying to be perfect. What areas of your life bring out your perfectionism the most?

1. You have an art project due at the end of the month. What's the best part?

a. Just getting it done

b. Brainstorming ideas and trying them out

c. Getting an A

2. Basketball tryouts are next week. Do you:

a. Hope you are good enough to make the team?

b. Practice some with friends, so you feel ready?

c. Stay out shooting baskets nonstop until dark every day?

3. You'll add a photo to your story only when:

a. It reminds you of a great time.

b. It looks like you are having fun.

c. You look just right.

4. What is the right number of friends on social media?

a. As long as your close friends are there, who cares?

b. It's nice when you can add some new people

c. More friends than everyone else

5. What do you think about after you turn in a quiz?

a. Nothing—it's already turned in.

b. You hope you did well, since you studied.

c. You go over the answers again in your head, getting frustrated with mistakes and convincing yourself you totally failed.

6. How do you feel when your parents come to watch your game?

a. I'm glad they're here to support me.

b. I hope I get a lot of playing time so they can watch me.

c. I absolutely have to score today.

7. How long does it take to get ready for school in the morning?

a. Five minutes—I just roll out.

b. Maybe 20 minutes, if I'm trying to find the perfect outfit.

c. At least 45 minutes to get everything right.

Answers:

How many Cs did you have in your answers? If the answer is more than two or three, you might be suffering from a bad case of perfectionism. Remember, when you try to do everything perfectly, you usually end up putting a lot more stress and pressure on yourself. Take a look at which questions you answered C to as well. If you answered C to #1 and #5, you may have some pressure academically. For #2 and #6, sports may be where you show your perfectionism. For #3 and #7, you might be stressed out about your appearance. And for #4, social media may be your trigger.

MAKE A LIST OF THINGS YOU FEEL LIKE YOU *should* DO BUT MIGHT NOT NECESSARILY *want* TO DO.

WHY DO YOU FEEL LIKE YOU SHOULD DO THOSE THINGS?

→

→

→

→

Get all As.

Make the basketball team.

what are some things that you do
JUST FOR YOURSELF,
not to make anyone else happy?

_____

_____

_____

_____

_____

_____

_____

_____

_____

_____

_____

_____

_____

_____

_____

outside of school, homework, chores, and other obligations, do you feel like you spend more of your time doing things to make yourself happy or to make other people happy? Why?

_____

_____

_____

_____

_____

_____

_____

_____

_____

_____

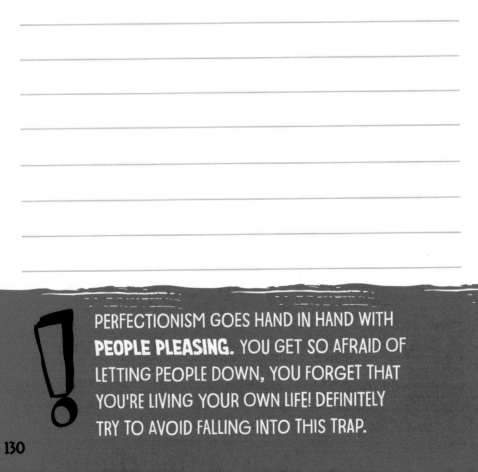

PERFECTIONISM GOES HAND IN HAND WITH **PEOPLE PLEASING.** YOU GET SO AFRAID OF LETTING PEOPLE DOWN, YOU FORGET THAT YOU'RE LIVING YOUR OWN LIFE! DEFINITELY TRY TO AVOID FALLING INTO THIS TRAP.

WRITE ABOUT A TIME WHEN ADULTS MADE YOU FEEL PRESSURED OR STRESSED WITH THEIR EXPECTATIONS, AND HOW IT MADE YOU FEEL.

**Go back to that list of perfectionism pressures on page 123.
Pick one to focus on for the next two pages.**

If you were trying to be absolutely perfect
at this, what would your goal be?

_____

_____

_____

_____

Is that a realistic, achievable goal?

_____

_____

Why do you think you want to do this
perfectly?

_____

_____

_____

_____

Now try setting a smaller goal you know you can reach. For example, if you feel pressured to always say the right thing, pick a time when you feel really comfortable, like with friends or at dinner at home, and practice saying exactly what you think without worrying about how it sounds. Give yourself a deadline—a day, two days, a week. Then do the best you can in that time limit and declare it "Good enough!"

Goal: _____

_____

_____

Does that goal feel more achievable?

_____

_____

Deadline: _____

Date completed: _____

How did it go?

_____

_____

IMAGINE IF YOU ONLY COMPARED YOURSELF . . . TO YOURSELF!
IF YOU LOOKED AT HOW MUCH BETTER YOU ARE AT THINGS THAN
YOU USED TO BE, INSTEAD OF HOW WELL SOMEONE ELSE DOES
THEM. DESCRIBE HOW YOU THINK YOUR LIFE WOULD BE DIFFERENT.

Do you ever put off things that you have to do, so that you end up starting them late? Why do you think you do that?

LOOK AT THE BOYS IN YOUR GRADE.
DO THEY SEEM LIKE THEY'RE TRYING TO BE PERFECT?

_____

_____

_____

_____

WHY DO YOU THINK PERFECTIONISM IS MORE
OF AN ISSUE FOR GIRLS THAN FOR BOYS?

_____

_____

_____

_____

_____

PERFECTIONISM USUALLY LEADS TO
procrastination.
WHEN YOU FEEL PRESSURE TO DO SOMETHING
PERFECTLY AND YOU'RE AFRAID OF FAILING, YOU'RE
SCARED TO EVEN TRY. SO YOU PUT IT OFF AND PUT
IT OFF—SOMETIMES UNTIL IT'S TOO LATE.

Next time you're procrastinating, what are some things you can tell yourself to make it easier to press pause on perfectionism and get started?

Keep this list handy for the next time you need it!

Don't wait until you **feel** like doing it. Just start doing it.

Break it down into smaller goals to make it easier.

If you had a whole day with absolutely nothing planned and nothing you had to do, how would you spend it?

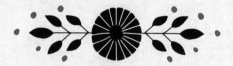

Perfectionism

CAN BE REALLY TOXIC WHEN WE OBSESS OVER HOW OTHERS THINK WE SHOULD LOOK.

WHILE IT'S GOOD TO LOVE WHAT YOU SEE IN THE MIRROR,

THE PRESSURE

TO LOOK LIKE EVERYONE ELSE

can feel overwhelming.

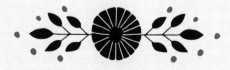

HOW IMPORTANT IS YOUR APPEARANCE TO YOU?

Circle one.

Not at all.

Pretty important.

A little.

A lot.

Sometimes a lot, sometimes not.

SUPER important.

DESCRIBE OR DRAW THE WAY YOU LOOK AND DRESS.

WHEN PEOPLE LOOK AT YOU, WHAT DO YOU MOST *WANT* THEM TO THINK?

Circle your top three.

strong

confident

Nice

Funny

Bold

Beautiful

cool

Talented

Smart

Popular

caring

Adventurous

Passionate

Athletic

creative

Fun

write about a time you were pressured to change how you look or dress, and how it felt.

_____

_____

_____

_____

_____

_____

_____

_____

_____

_____

_____

_____

_____

_____

MAKE A LIST OF THINGS YOU LIKE ABOUT YOUR APPEARANCE AND THE WAY YOU DRESS!

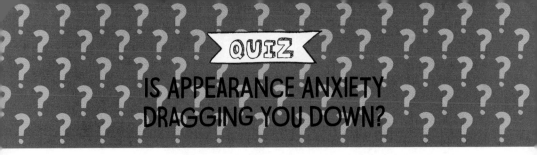

IS APPEARANCE ANXIETY DRAGGING YOU DOWN?

Everyone worries about their looks. Even the most gorgeous supermodel, even the most popular YouTube star, even Beyoncé. But is this worry stopping you from living the life you want? Circle either yes or no below to learn more.

1. **Do you not believe your friends when they give you a compliment?**

    Yes   No

2. **Do you have a feature or a body part you hate?**

    Yes   No

3. **Do you ever avoid looking in the mirror?**

    Yes   No

4. **Do you compare your looks to your friends' looks a lot?**

    Yes   No

5. **Do you feel more attractive if you are wearing certain brands or logos?**

    Yes   No

6. Do you avoid posting photos on social media if you don't look perfect?

7. If you were invited to a pool party, would you worry about wearing a bathing suit in front of your friends?

8. If someone teased you about your shirt, would you stop wearing it?

Yes   No

9. If you had a big pimple on your face, would you stay home from school?

Yes   No

10. Do you feel like everyone can tell when you are having a bad hair day?

Answers:

If you answered Yes to five or more of the questions, how you feel about the way you look may be holding you back. If you wait until you look absolutely perfect to do things, you'll end up waiting your entire life!

Go back to your list of role models on page 17. Do you think these women worry more about their appearance or what they do?

_____

_____

_____

_____

Do some digging. Can you find any stories about those women doubting themselves because of the way they look? You'd be surprised to find that even senators and supermodels worry about their appearance.

_____

_____

_____

_____

_____

WHEN YOU POST PHOTOS ONLINE, DO YOU WORRY A LOT ABOUT HOW YOU LOOK IN THEM? WRITE DOWN SOME OF THOSE WORRIES BELOW.

How do you think people treat appearance differently for boys and for girls?

cut out some photos from magazines (or bookmark photos online) that look like people you know in real life. Were these pictures harder or easier to find than you thought they would be?

LIST FIVE STYLE ROLE MODELS—PEOPLE WHO DRESS
HOW THEY WANT, IN A WAY THAT REFLECTS THEIR TRUE
AUTHENTIC SELVES, NO MATTER WHAT OTHER PEOPLE SAY.

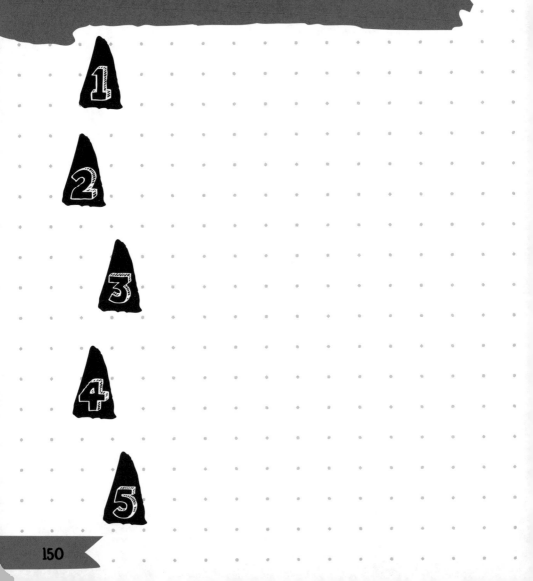

1

2

3

4

5

BEING 100%,

fully, truly, utterly yourself

IS A BIG PART OF CONFIDENCE.

But who are you, anyway?

Sometimes, the answer
might seem obvious.
At other moments,

THE REAL YOU

might feel like a puzzle with
a lot of missing pieces.

HOW would your best friend describe you?

HOW would your family describe you?

HOW would you describe you?

HOW OFTEN DO YOU FEEL LIKE YOU'RE A DIFFERENT PERSON WITH DIFFERENT PEOPLE?

In 10 years, you'll mostly be a different person. Describe your future self and what you hope you'll be like.

Values are your beliefs, the ideas that matter most to you and help shape how you behave. Things like honesty, compassion, creativity, etc. They make up a big part of who you are.

Make a list of values that are important to you.

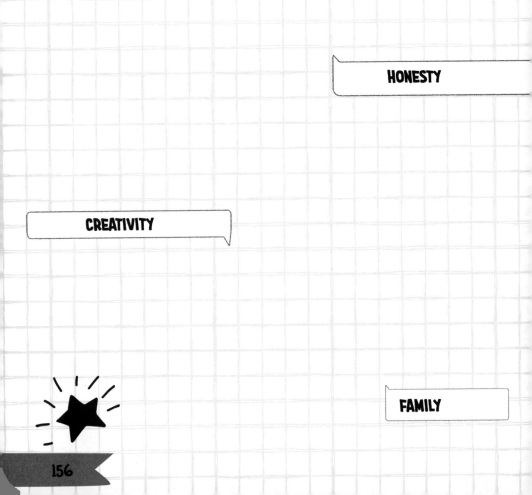

HONESTY

CREATIVITY

FAMILY

ANOTHER WAY TO FIGURE OUT WHO YOU ARE IS TO THINK ABOUT YOUR TRUE STRENGTHS. ANSWER THESE QUESTIONS TO HELP YOU DISCOVER WHAT THOSE ARE.

What makes you feel good while you are doing it?

What gives you energy?

What do you do that makes you happy?

What do you do a lot, on your own, without ever being reminded?

What kind of things do you notice in the world?

What kind of things make you excited?

What kind of things cause you to lose track of time?

NOW MAKE A LIST OF ALL YOUR TRUE STRENGTHS!

An ability is a true strength when

- ◆ You're pretty good at it.
- ◆ You're passionate about it (no one has to nag you to do it).
- ◆ It brings you joy (you often lose track of time while doing it).

LOOK AT YOUR VALUES ON PAGE 156 AND YOUR STRENGTHS ON PAGE 158. HOW DO THEY FIT TOGETHER? WHAT DO YOU THINK THESE LISTS SAY ABOUT YOUR PERSONALITY?

BASED ON YOUR LISTS OF STRENGTHS AND VALUES, DO YOU FEEL LIKE YOU ARE YOUR MOST AUTHENTIC SELF MOST OF THE TIME? IF NOT, WHAT DO YOU THINK IS HOLDING YOU BACK?

WHEN DO YOU FEEL THE MOST LIKE YOURSELF?

RATE EACH OF THESE PLACES 1 TO 5, WITH ONE MEANING YOU ACT **nothing** LIKE YOUR MOST AUTHENTIC SELF AND FIVE MEANING YOU ACT **completely** LIKE YOURSELF.

At school, in class
1 2 3 4 5

At school, at lunch
1 2 3 4 5

With my friends
1 2 3 4 5

Alone in my room
1 2 3 4 5

With my family
1 2 3 4 5

During other activities like plays, clubs, or music
1 2 3 4 5

While playing sports
1 2 3 4 5

WHEN DO YOU FEEL THE **most** LIKE THE TRUE, AUTHENTIC VERSION OF YOU? WHY?

WHEN DO YOU FEEL THE **least** LIKE THE TRUE, AUTHENTIC VERSION OF YOU? WHY?

What do you think would happen if you tried to be true to you in every situation, no matter where you were or who you were with? Would your life change at all?

QUIZ

HOW WELL DO YOU DO YOU?

Take the quiz below to see!

1. A few of your friends invite you to go see a band you don't like. Do you:

a. Pay for the ticket and go anyway?

b. Bow out—there will be other shows?

2. You meet a bunch of kids on vacation who like surfing, which you've never done. Do you:

a. Nod along when they talk about it, hoping they assume you've surfed?

b. Ask questions about it because it sounds amazing and you're curious?

3. It's getting really late at a sleepover but some of the other girls are still wide awake. Do you:

a. Force yourself to stay up so you don't miss anything?

b. Roll over and get some sleep, figuring you'll catch up in the morning?

4. You see a hairstyle on Instagram that is a little dramatic but you think will look good on you. Do you:

a. Run it by your friends to see if they like it?

b. Try it out—it's only hair?

5. **You've had a terrible day and someone at the lunch table asks what's wrong. Do you:**

   a. Smile and say nothing's wrong, you're fine?

   b. Tell them about your rotten day?

6. **Your class is reading a book you love but no one else seems to like. Do you:**

   a. Avoid talking about the book in class but ace the quiz?

   b. Raise your hand so you can make the case for why it's awesome?

7. **You were looking at your phone and missed the last-minute shot that won the game. Do you:**

   a. Act like you saw it because it's all anyone is talking about?

   b. Ask your friend to describe what happened?

8. **One of your friends is really funny and loud. When you hang out together, do you:**

   a. Find yourself getting caught up in her personality, making more jokes than you normally do?

   b. Enjoy being around her but realize it's just not you to be that way?

Answers:

If you answered B to most of these questions, you tend to act the same no matter where you are. If you answered A to more than four, you might be a social chameleon. It's okay to act differently in different situations, but when you try to alter your personality to fit in, your confidence levels end up taking a hit. Give the world a chance to meet the real you—you'll be surprised at how good it makes you feel!

DRAW A PICTURE OR WRITE ABOUT HOW YOU WOULD DRESS AND BEHAVE IN AN IDEAL WORLD WHERE ABSOLUTELY NO ONE JUDGED YOU.

!

ONE MAJOR WAY TO BE TRUE TO YOURSELF IS LOOKING LIKE YOURSELF. THERE'S NO RIGHT OR WRONG STYLE. IF YOU USE YOUR CLOTHES TO EXPRESS YOURSELF, THEN YOU ARE THE ONLY ONE WHO HAS TO LIKE THEM.

Do you feel like who you are on the inside matches who you are on the outside? Why or why not?

_____

_____

_____

_____

_____

_____

_____

_____

_____

_____

_____

If you could give your younger self advice, what would you say?

>>>>>>>>>>>>>>>>>>>>>>>>>>>

PART OF YOUR ABILITY TO FEEL

CONFIDENT

DOESN'T COME FROM INSIDE YOU.

IT COMES FROM THE WAY THE WORLD WORKS
AND HOW THAT AFFECTS YOU—

★ THE CULTURE. ★

culture is powerful—
it affects the way we

think & act.

SOMETIMES YOU CAN CHANGE THE CULTURE.

But the most important thing to do
is notice it.

>>>>>>>>>>>>>>>>>>>>>>>>>>>

Look at the list of adjectives below. circle the ones that people most often use to describe boys in one color and girls in another color.

STRONG   FAST

BOLD   SMART

PRETTY   EMOTIONAL

SWEET   FUNNY

QUIET   FRIENDLY

SHY   KIND

GOOD   DELICATE

ENERGETIC   SILLY

OUTGOING   TOUGH

HOW ARE THE ONES FOR BOYS DIFFERENT FROM THE ONES FOR GIRLS?

HOW DO YOU THINK IT MAKES GIRLS FEEL TO BE THOUGHT OF THAT WAY?

HOW DO YOU THINK IT MAKES BOYS FEEL?

THERE ARE SOME OLD-FASHIONED ASSUMPTIONS OUT THERE THAT GIRLS ARE SOMEHOW WEAKER, OR LESS COMPETITIVE, OR SILLIER THAN BOYS. DON'T BELIEVE IT FOR A SECOND! GIRLS ARE AS STRONG AND POWERFUL, AND AS GOOD AS (AND OFTEN EVEN BETTER THAN) BOYS AT ALL KINDS OF STUFF.

DO YOU THINK HAVING CONFIDENCE IS THE SAME OR
HARDER FOR GIRLS THAN BOYS? WHY?

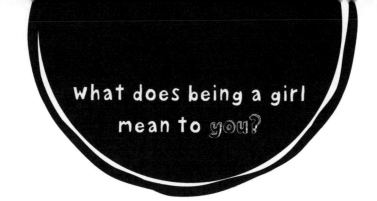

what does being a girl
mean to you?

_____

_____

_____

_____

_____

_____

_____

_____

_____

_____

THERE ARE AN INFINITE NUMBER OF WAYS TO BE A GIRL. THERE'S NO RIGHT WAY FOR GIRLS TO ACT OR BE.

MAKE A LIST OF WHAT YOU LIKE ABOUT BEING A GIRL.

WHAT ARE SOME THINGS THAT ARE HARD ABOUT BEING A GIRL?

✗

✗

✗

✗

✗

✗

✗

✗

✗

✗

Think about the situations below. There are no right or wrong answers in this quiz—it's just a way to help you think about the culture and how it affects you.

1. Is there any career you feel like you can't do because you're female?

   Yes   Maybe   No

2. Should male and female sports stars be paid the same?

   Yes   Maybe   No

3. Can a female pop star be popular if she isn't pretty?

   Yes   Maybe   No

4. Do boys have the same definition of perfect as girls?

   Yes   Maybe   No

5. Are superhero movies made for girls?

   Yes   Maybe   No

6. Is it possible for you to look like models in magazines?

Yes   Maybe   No

7. Is it an insult when someone says "you throw like a girl"?

Yes   Maybe   No

8. Do you know people who wouldn't vote for a woman for president?

Yes   Maybe   No

9. Are you ever afraid to walk by a group of boys on your own?

Yes   Maybe   No

10. Do you think having trendy clothes will make you more popular?

Yes   Maybe   No

Take a look at some newspapers, magazines, movies, TV, and songs. Write down some examples of how girls and women are described or shown versus how boys and men are described or shown.

WOMEN

MEN

Sometimes, you might get treated differently because of stereotypes about your gender, race, ability or disability, religion, where you live, or your sexual identity. A stereotype is when someone assumes that all people in a group are alike.

Have you ever been stereotyped? How did it feel?

HAVE YOU EVER STEREOTYPED ANYONE?

Describe what happened and why you might have jumped to conclusions.

Brainstorm some ways you can start to change the culture around you for the better! Whether it's calling out a classmate who thinks girls should be quieter than boys or pointing out stereotypes in a textbook. The more people realize what needs to change, the easier it will be for everyone to be themselves.

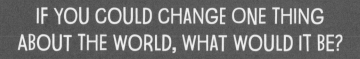

IF YOU COULD CHANGE ONE THING ABOUT THE WORLD, WHAT WOULD IT BE?

Helping others is a great way to

BUILD CONFIDENCE.

Switching your circuits from

ME thinking to WE thinking

gives you a

happiness boost

and increases your confidence.

WHY?

Researchers have found it gets you
over the hurdle of being

TOO SELF-CONSCIOUS

about taking a risk
or action.

Write about a time you helped someone or volunteered, and how it made you feel.

CONFIDENCE IS A CYCLE. ACTION BUILDS CONFIDENCE. CONFIDENCE HELPS US TAKE ACTION. BUT SOMETIMES IT CAN BE HARD TO GET THAT CYCLE STARTED. IT HELPS TO HAVE A MANTRA, A PHRASE YOU CAN REPEAT WHEN YOU NEED A CONFIDENCE BOOST TO TAKE THAT FIRST STEP.

come up with a confidence mantra
and write it below.

Make a list of people or causes you can help! Starting a club at school to fight climate change, helping a friend with her homework—anything that makes you feel excited and motivated.

volunteering with animals.

Raising money for the girls' cross-country team.

CAN YOU THINK OF WAYS TO HELP PEOPLE AND CAUSES THAT
RELATE TO YOUR STRENGTHS AND VALUES FROM PAGES 156
AND 158? IF YOU ALIGN YOUR VALUES AND STRENGTHS WITH A
CAUSE YOU BELIEVE IN, NOTHING WILL BE ABLE TO STOP YOU!

WHEN ACTION GETS REALLY BIG AND HAS
a deeper purpose,
IT'S CALLED activism.

Pick a cause from your list on page 186 and brainstorm some things you can do to help.

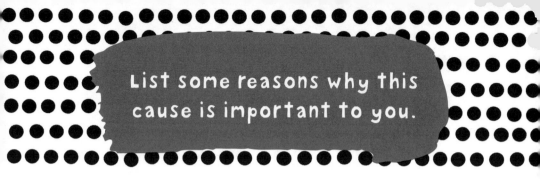

List some reasons why this cause is important to you.

_____

_____

_____

_____

_____

_____

_____

_____

_____

_____

_____

_____

IF YOU'RE GOING TO FIGHT FOR A CAUSE, YOU HAVE TO LEARN TO SPEAK CONFIDENTLY ABOUT IT.

Are you good at speaking in front of other people?

How often do you apologize for speaking up or for things that aren't your fault?

Do you ever make fun of yourself to make sure you don't seem stuck up? Why?

YOU ARE POWERFUL, SO YOUR WORDS NEED TO MATCH.

Look at the examples of unconfident speech below. Do any of them seem familiar? Now come up with stronger, more active ways to say the same thing without saying sorry or putting yourself down. Don't worry about seeming too direct or bold—that's the point!

"This may be a stupid question . . ."

"Excuse me, sorry, I hate to bother you . . ."

"Um, is this project okay? I'm not sure."

"I only scored the winning goal because I got lucky."

"What do you want to do? I don't care, whatever's fine."

"I'm sorry, I actually ordered a chocolate milk shake, not strawberry."

"I might be wrong, but isn't the answer actually . . ."

DO YOU SPEAK YOUR MIND?

1. When you are asked what you want to do for your birthday, do you say:

a. What you think everyone else would like to do?

b. Nothing—you don't want to be any trouble?

c. What would make you truly happy?

2. A kid you don't really like asks you to hang out. Do you:

a. Say yes reluctantly—you don't want to hurt anyone's feelings?

b. Make up an elaborate excuse?

c. Say no, but invite him to hang out in a group instead?

3. You have a group project in science class. The rest of your group wants to make a volcano, but you think that's been done too many times and will be boring. Do you:

a. Go along with the group—majority rules?

b. Tell one person what you think and hope they tell the group?

c. Talk to the group about your concerns?

4. You are with your friends and a waitress brings you the wrong burger. Do you:

a. Eat it—it's fine?

b. Complain to your friends but don't make a big deal?

c. Get the waitress's attention and explain she made a mistake?

5. You get a quiz back and the teacher marked an answer wrong that is right. Do you:

a. Let it go—it doesn't affect your grade much?

b. Tell your mom and hope she fixes it?

c. Talk to the teacher after class about her error?

Answers: If you answered mainly **A**s, you're focusing more on pleasing other people than on making yourself happy. If you answered mainly **B**s, you know you have something to say but you're having trouble finding the confidence to say it. If you answered mainly **C**s, you're finding ways to speak up about how you feel.

A CONFIDENT GIRL'S
MANIFESTO

I have the right to be treated with respect.

I have the right to boundaries
and personal space.

I will speak up or take action when someone or
something is making me uncomfortable.

I don't always please people—
that's not my job.

I am loyal to friends and family, but also to
myself and my values, to doing the right thing.

I am strong enough to deal with the
consequences of actions I take.

I will find a trusted adult
when I need help.

LOOK AT THE CONFIDENCE MANIFESTO ON THE PREVIOUS PAGE.

HOW DOES IT MAKE YOU FEEL?

DO YOU AGREE WITH ALL OF THOSE STATEMENTS? WHY OR WHY NOT?

Do any of the statements in the manifesto feel more important to you than others?

Why?

LIST THE THINGS YOU CAN DO TO TURN THESE CONFIDENCE STATEMENTS INTO ACTIONS.

_____

_____

_____

_____

_____

_____

_____

_____

_____

_____

_____

_____

_____

_____

Write your own personalized
Confidence Manifesto
that's specific to your life and goals.

_____

_____

_____

_____

_____

_____

_____

_____

_____

_____

_____

_____

_____

_____

Describe five unexpected things you learned about yourself through the pages of this journal.

You've probably realized by now, but confidence is **awesome.** Having confidence will let you do all the fun, exciting things that you want to do. And confidence is something that you'll keep building your entire life.

One great way to build it is through **The confidence code.** It's a mantra backed up by scientific research that can help girls and women create confidence. And it's made up of three big elements.

- **Risk More**
- **Think Less**
- **Be Yourself**

NOW IT'S TIME TO BUILD YOUR OWN CONFIDENCE CODE.
TO HELP YOU BRAINSTORM, YOU CAN ALSO TRY THINKING
ABOUT IT THIS WAY:

I will _____

I won't _____

I am _____

Take what you brainstormed and turn it into three phrases that will remind you to stay confident. Think of actions you want to take, areas that are particularly challenging for you, or a mantra that inspires you. Then plug it into the confidence code shield below and decorate it.

Your Confidence Code will change and morph over time. Day to day, week to week, it might look completely different, and that's okay. Once your confidence starts growing, your Confidence Code will need to adapt.

That's why we've given you lots of blank Confidence Code shields at the end of this book. Decorate them however you like and add your name at the bottom. Fill one out, cut it out, and tape it up where you can see it. Then, whenever you're ready for a new code, turn it over and fill out the other side. Keep your code front and center all the time. Eventually, following the code will become as instinctive as a muscle memory, as natural as riding a bike, reading a book, or texting on your phone.

Go make your own confidence code
and let your confident life begin!